PIERCE BROSNAN

The Man with the Golden Charm

ETHAN REYNOLDS

Copyright © 2025 by ETHAN REYNOLDS

All rights reserved. No part of this publication may be reproduced, distributed, or transmitted in any form or by any means, including photocopying, recording, or other electronic or mechanical methods, without the prior written permission of the publisher, except in the case of brief quotations embodied in critical reviews and certain other noncommercial uses permitted by copyright law.

Table of Contents

Introduction 6
   An Overview of Pierce Brosnan's Significance in Film and Culture 6

Chapter 1: Early Life and Formative Years 15
   Childhood in Ireland and England 15
   Family Dynamics and Early Influences 21

Chapter 2: Discovering the Stage. 28
   Journey into Acting 29
   Training at the Drama Centre London 34

Chapter 3: Breakthrough with Remington Steele 41
   Landing the Titular Role 41
   Impact on His Career Trajectory 45

Chapter 4: Personal Triumphs and Tragedies. 51
   Marriage to Cassandra Harris 51
   Navigating Personal Loss and Resilience 57

Chapter 5: Becoming Bond. 63
   The Road to Portraying James Bond 63
   Analysis of His Performances in GoldenEye, Tomorrow Never Dies, The

World Is Not Enough, and Die Another Day   68

Chapter 6: Beyond 007   76
Diversifying Roles: The Thomas Crown Affair and Dante's Peak   76

Exploring His Range in Different Genres   81

Chapter 7: Personal Life and Advocacy   91
Family Life with Keely Shaye Smith and Children   91

Environmental Activism and Philanthropic Endeavors   92

Chapter 8: Later Career and Recent Works   95
Roles in Mamma Mia!, The Matador, and Black Adam   95

Continued Presence in the Entertainment Industry   101

Chapter 9: Legacy and Influence.   108
Impact on Cinema and Future Actors   108

Reflections on a Storied Career   113

conclusion   120
Filmography   126
Awards and Honors   131

Industry Recognition 131
Major Award Nominations and Wins 132
Impact on Future Generations 136

Introduction

An Overview of Pierce Brosnan's Significance in Film and Culture

Pierce Brosnan's name evokes an era of suave sophistication and cinematic excellence that continues to resonate across generations. Born in 1953 in Drogheda, Ireland, Brosnan's journey from a modest beginning to becoming one of Hollywood's most celebrated actors is a narrative of resilience, reinvention, and unwavering charm. His evolution as a performer is not merely the chronicle of a man stepping into the spotlight but a reflection of cultural shifts in the portrayal of masculinity, heroism, and style on the global stage. Over the decades, Brosnan has come to embody the archetype of the modern leading man—a combination of rugged good looks, intellectual depth, and an unassuming yet magnetic presence that has redefined what it means to be a movie star in an era marked by both tradition and transformation.

At the heart of Brosnan's significance is his tenure as James Bond, a role that has not only cemented his legacy in film history but also redefined a cultural icon. When he first donned the tuxedo in GoldenEye (1995), Brosnan stepped into a lineage of Bond actors and reimagined the character for a new generation. His Bond was not merely a gadget-wielding secret agent; he was a man who balanced charm with grit, wit with wisdom, and a touch of vulnerability amidst the high-octane action. Brosnan's portrayal resonated with audiences around the world, blending the classic sophistication associated with Bond with a contemporary edge that made the character both timeless and relevant. In doing so, he not only revitalized the franchise but also influenced how cinematic heroes would be portrayed in the years to follow.

Beyond the Bond films, Brosnan's career has been marked by a diverse array of roles that reflect his versatility and willingness to embrace both mainstream blockbusters and more nuanced, character-driven projects. From his early television work in Remington Steele—a series that itself became a cultural phenomenon—to dramatic performances in films like The Thomas Crown Affair and action-packed ventures such as Tomorrow Never Dies, Brosnan's body of work demonstrates an adaptability that has allowed him to traverse genres seamlessly. This ability to oscillate between different modes of storytelling is significant because it mirrors the evolving tastes of audiences, who increasingly seek multifaceted characters and narratives that break away from one-dimensional portrayals. In this way, Brosnan's career can be seen as a microcosm of the broader changes within the film industry, where innovation and tradition coexist and inform one another.

Pierce Brosnan's appeal extends far beyond the silver screen. His personal style—marked by an effortless elegance and an unpretentious demeanor—has had a lasting impact on popular culture. In an industry often characterized by fleeting trends and the relentless pursuit of novelty, Brosnan's consistency as a symbol of refined masculinity has rendered him a timeless figure. Whether he is seen on the red carpet in impeccably tailored suits or engaging in philanthropic endeavors offscreen, his image is one of dignified charm and quiet determination. This cultivated persona has, in many ways, helped to redefine the standards of celebrity in contemporary culture. Rather than relying solely on the glitz and glamour that define much of Hollywood's visual culture, Brosnan's enduring legacy is built on the foundations of substance, authenticity, and a deep understanding of the human experience.

Culturally, Brosnan's influence can also be seen in his approach to the art of storytelling. His work often explores themes of redemption, moral complexity, and the eternal struggle between personal ambition and collective responsibility. Whether in his roles as an international spy, a con artist with a heart of gold, or a man confronting his personal demons, Brosnan has consistently sought to portray characters that are as intellectually engaging as they are visually captivating. This intellectual curiosity has fostered a dialogue between audiences and filmmakers, encouraging a more reflective engagement with the narratives presented on screen. In a time when films are increasingly recognized not just as sources of entertainment but as vehicles for social commentary and personal introspection, Brosnan's filmography serves as a testament to the power of cinema to mirror and shape cultural values.

Moreover, Pierce Brosnan's contributions are not confined to his onscreen work alone. His offscreen life—marked by his commitment to environmental causes, his advocacy for cancer awareness, and his support of various philanthropic initiatives—demonstrates a broader understanding of the role that public figures can play in society. In an era when celebrities are often scrutinized for their personal choices, Brosnan has used his platform to promote meaningful change. His activism and charitable work offer a counterpoint to the often superficial nature of celebrity culture, reminding us that true influence is measured not only by one's professional achievements but also by the positive impact one has on the world. This multidimensional approach to his career and life has earned him respect not only as an actor but as a global citizen dedicated to fostering a better, more sustainable future.

The narrative of Pierce Brosnan's life is interwoven with the historical and cultural developments of his time. Coming of age during the transformative decades of the late 20th century, he experienced firsthand the rapid evolution of the film industry—a period marked by technological innovation, changing social mores, and the globalization of cinema. His ability to adapt to these changes while maintaining his unique personal style speaks to a broader cultural narrative: the persistence of quality and authenticity in an ever-changing world. His success illustrates how timeless talent, when combined with a willingness to evolve, can leave an indelible mark on both the artistic and cultural landscapes.

One cannot overlook the significance of Brosnan's Irish heritage in understanding his cultural impact. In an industry dominated by American narratives, his Irish background provides a rich, distinctive perspective that has contributed to his universal appeal. The blend of Celtic charm with a cosmopolitan sensibility has helped Brosnan forge a unique identity that transcends national borders. His success has not only elevated him as an individual actor but has also served as a source of pride for the Irish community, inspiring countless aspiring actors to pursue their dreams regardless of their origins. This dual identity—rooted in his cultural heritage yet embracing the global stage—embodies the spirit of a truly modern artist.

In reflecting on Pierce Brosnan's significance, it is essential to consider the broader impact of his work on future generations of actors and filmmakers. His innovative approach to character development and his commitment to exploring complex, multidimensional narratives have set a benchmark for excellence in acting. Young actors looking to break into the industry often cite Brosnan's performances as both inspirational and instructive, providing a blueprint for how to navigate the intricacies of a long and varied career. His legacy is not simply measured by box office numbers or award counts, but by the enduring influence he has had on the craft of acting itself—a craft that prizes authenticity, nuance, and a relentless pursuit of artistic excellence.

Furthermore, the technological advancements in filmmaking during Brosnan's career have also played a role in amplifying his influence. From the practical effects of the 1980s to the digital innovations of today, his films have mirrored the technological transformations of their times. Brosnan's willingness to engage with new storytelling techniques and his openness to experimenting with different cinematic styles have made him a pioneer in embracing the future of film. This symbiotic relationship between an actor and the evolving medium of cinema is a key component of his cultural significance. It underscores the idea that great art is not static but is continually reshaped by the innovations and challenges of its era.

As we examine the multifaceted legacy of Pierce Brosnan, it becomes evident that his contributions extend far beyond the confines of his filmography. His life story, marked by both extraordinary successes and personal challenges, serves as an enduring source of inspiration. In a world where the lines between art and life are increasingly blurred, Brosnan's ability to maintain a sense of integrity and authenticity—both on and off screen—reminds us that true artistry is defined by its capacity to touch lives and provoke thought. His journey from a young actor in a burgeoning television series to a global icon of film is a narrative of perseverance, passion, and the relentless pursuit of excellence.

In conclusion, Pierce Brosnan's significance in film and culture is as multifaceted as it is profound. His portrayal of James Bond redefined an iconic character for a new era, his diverse body of work continues to challenge and captivate audiences, and his offscreen contributions remind us of the power of celebrity when wielded with purpose and responsibility. Brosnan's enduring legacy is a testament to his ability to navigate the ever-changing currents of popular culture while staying true to the timeless qualities of authenticity, sophistication, and human warmth. For anyone interested in the interplay between cinema, culture, and personal identity, the life and career of Pierce Brosnan offer rich insights into the art of storytelling and the enduring impact of a truly remarkable artist.

Chapter 1: Early Life and Formative Years

Childhood in Ireland and England

Pierce Brosnan's early years unfolded against a backdrop of contrasting landscapes and cultural milieus that would ultimately define his creative spirit. Born on May 16, 1953, in Drogheda, County Louth, Ireland, Brosnan entered a world where the rugged beauty of the Irish countryside was interwoven with centuries of myth, music, and literary tradition. This small town setting, steeped in history and community spirit, provided a formative canvas for the young boy whose later career would come to embody a blend of classic charm and modern sophistication.

In Ireland, the rhythms of everyday life were punctuated by local traditions and storytelling—a heritage that has long celebrated the oral tradition and the arts. As a child, Brosnan was immersed in an environment where community gatherings, local music sessions, and tales of heroic feats were a part of daily life. These experiences, though subtle, planted the seeds of a lifelong appreciation for narrative and performance. The cadence of the Irish language, the evocative folklore, and the inherent connection to the land all contributed to an early sense of identity and belonging.

Yet, like many of his generation, Brosnan's life would soon be touched by the transformative influence of migration. His family's eventual move from Ireland to England signified not only a geographical shift but also the beginning of a dynamic cultural integration. In England, the young Pierce found himself navigating a new educational system, social norms, and a broader, more cosmopolitan environment. This transition from the insular familiarity of an Irish town to the bustling urban life in England was both challenging and exhilarating. It offered him a chance to engage with a diversity of ideas and artistic expressions that would later be evident in his varied career choices.

The contrasting worlds of Ireland and England provided Brosnan with a unique duality in perspective. In Ireland, he absorbed the poetic melancholy and rugged resilience of a nation that had weathered centuries of hardship and triumph. In England, he encountered the modernity and innovation of a country that was rapidly evolving into a global cultural hub. This blend of tradition and modernity became a recurring motif in his life. The artistic sensibilities nurtured by the Irish milieu—its storytelling, its music, its emphasis on the oral and the imaginative—were complemented by the structured, progressive influences he encountered in England. Together, these experiences enriched his creative palette, enabling him to later embody characters with both depth and an air of refined sophistication.

During his school years in England, Brosnan's exposure to theatre and the performing arts began to take root. English schools, with their robust extracurricular programs and an emphasis on drama, offered him his first taste of the stage. It was in these early years that the spark of performance ignited. Whether it was participating in school plays or engaging in local community theatre, the stage became a space where he could explore and express his evolving identity. The discipline of learning lines, the thrill of live performance, and the camaraderie shared with fellow actors instilled in him an enduring passion for storytelling—a passion that would later propel him into the limelight of international cinema.

Moreover, the move to England during his formative years presented a unique set of challenges. Adapting to a new accent, making new friends, and reconciling the differences between his Irish roots and his new English surroundings demanded resilience and adaptability. These experiences, though often fraught with the uncertainties typical of childhood transitions, helped shape his character. They taught him the value of perseverance and the importance of embracing change—lessons that would prove invaluable throughout his multifaceted career in film and beyond.

Brosnan's childhood is also marked by an evolving sense of self that was informed by both the community and the wider world. In Ireland, the collective memory of past struggles and triumphs lent a weight and gravitas to everyday conversations. In England, the exposure to a more diverse and competitive environment provided the impetus to hone his unique talents and to distinguish himself. It was in this crucible of cultural intersection that he began to see himself not just as a product of his environment but as someone capable of bridging different worlds—a quality that would later define his persona both on and off screen.

As he grew older, the lessons gleaned from his early years in both Ireland and England began to coalesce into a broader understanding of art and identity. The rich tapestry of Irish folklore, with its heroes, legends, and poetic introspection, merged with the pragmatic, forward-thinking ethos of post-war England. This synthesis not only enriched his worldview but also laid the groundwork for the multifaceted characters he would later portray. In interviews and reflective writings, Brosnan has often alluded to the formative impact of these early experiences—a melding of the mystical and the modern that continues to inform his approach to both life and art.

In retrospect, Pierce Brosnan's childhood represents a microcosm of the transformative power of cultural exchange. It is a testament to how geographical relocation can serve as a catalyst for personal growth and creative expression. His journey from the enchanting streets of Drogheda to the vibrant urban centers of England encapsulates a broader narrative of resilience, adaptability, and the relentless pursuit of excellence. The influence of these early experiences is evident not only in the roles he later chose but also in the underlying themes of identity, belonging, and transformation that recur throughout his work.

In summary, the chapter of Brosnan's early years—spanning the lush, storied landscapes of Ireland and the dynamic, evolving environments of England—is a rich narrative of cultural interplay. It is a narrative that underscores the importance of heritage, the impact of new beginnings, and the enduring influence of early artistic exposure. These experiences, woven together, provided the raw material for a creative journey that would ultimately redefine the archetype of the modern cinematic hero.

Family Dynamics and Early Influences

The family environment in which Pierce Brosnan was raised played a pivotal role in shaping both his character and his future aspirations. While the specifics of his family life have been carefully guarded, the contours of his early home life reveal a story of resilience, deep-rooted values, and an unwavering commitment to the arts that can be traced back to his formative years.

Pierce Brosnan was born into a family that, despite facing economic and personal challenges, imbued him with a sense of determination and a passion for storytelling. His father, Thomas Brosnan, worked in a profession that required him to interact with a diverse range of people—a role that, while demanding, also exposed young Pierce to the broader tapestry of human experience. Whether through the casual conversations during family gatherings or the subtle lessons of responsibility and work ethic observed at home, these early interactions laid a foundation for Brosnan's understanding of human nature. His father's role, characterized by both its routine and its moments of unexpected insight, provided a window into the complexities of adult life—a complexity that Pierce would later masterfully translate into his multifaceted on-screen personas.

Equally influential was Brosnan's mother, whose nurturing spirit and deep commitment to family values helped shape his early perceptions of love, care, and resilience. Her role extended far beyond that of a traditional homemaker; she was a storyteller, a guardian of cultural traditions, and a constant source of emotional support. In an era when family narratives were passed down orally, the stories and anecdotes shared at home resonated deeply with young Pierce, instilling in him a belief in the power of narrative to transform and uplift. The values she imparted—empathy, kindness, and an unwavering sense of integrity—became integral to his personal and professional identity. It was through her gentle guidance that he learned to appreciate the nuanced interplay between strength and vulnerability, a balance that has come to define his approach to both life and his craft.

Family dynamics during Brosnan's early years were further complicated by the challenges inherent in reconciling the cultural differences between his Irish origins and his later life in England. Within this transitional context, the family unit served as a stabilizing force. The traditions of his Irish heritage—celebrated through festive gatherings, music, and folklore—continued to thrive at home, even as the family adapted to the new cultural norms encountered in England. This blending of traditions created a unique household culture where stories of Irish heroes and legends were told alongside the modern narratives of an evolving Britain. For a young Pierce, these dual narratives offered a rich tapestry of influences, each contributing to his growing sense of self. The constant interplay between the old and the new, the traditional and the modern, fostered an environment in which creativity and introspection could flourish.

In many ways, Brosnan's family life was emblematic of the broader societal shifts occurring during his youth. The tensions between tradition and modernity were not confined to the external world but were also reflected in the intimate spaces of the home. Conversations around the dinner table often revolved around topics that spanned the gamut—from the enduring legacy of Irish folklore to the pressing challenges of contemporary life in post-war England. This intellectual and emotional diversity was instrumental in broadening his horizons, encouraging him to think critically about the world and his place within it. Such discussions not only nurtured his budding interest in the arts but also laid the groundwork for the empathetic and nuanced characters he would later portray on screen.

Beyond the immediate family, the extended network of relatives and close family friends also played a significant role in shaping Brosnan's early influences. These figures, often steeped in tradition and local lore, contributed additional layers of meaning to his understanding of identity and heritage. Whether through shared celebrations of cultural festivals, the retelling of ancestral stories, or the simple act of communal support during trying times, these relationships underscored the importance of community and belonging. For a young Pierce, every interaction was a lesson in humanity—a lesson that would later be echoed in his portrayals of characters who, despite their glamorous exteriors, were deeply human at their core.

Moreover, the early exposure to art and performance within the family context cannot be understated. Family gatherings were frequently punctuated by moments of spontaneous performance—be it the recitation of poetry, the singing of traditional ballads, or the enactment of local legends. Such experiences fostered an early appreciation for the dramatic arts and nurtured a desire to communicate and connect through performance. The subtle lessons of timing, emotion, and storytelling gleaned from these moments would serve as the bedrock upon which Brosnan built his illustrious career.

The resilience instilled in him by his family, combined with the rich tapestry of cultural narratives to which he was exposed, set the stage for his later accomplishments. Facing the challenges of integrating two distinct cultural identities at a young age, he learned to navigate complexities with a calm determination—a quality that would become one of his signature traits in his public persona. The nurturing yet dynamic environment at home not only allowed him to develop a robust moral compass but also encouraged him to pursue excellence in every endeavor.

In reflecting on these early influences, one can discern the deep interplay between personal history and artistic expression in Pierce Brosnan's life. The values, stories, and lessons imparted by his family continue to reverberate in his work, whether through the quiet intensity of his dramatic performances or the effortless charm he exudes in lighter roles. His family dynamics, marked by both tenderness and tenacity, provided him with the emotional tools necessary to portray a wide range of characters—each imbued with the authenticity and complexity that audiences have come to expect.

In essence, the early family experiences of Pierce Brosnan are a testament to the transformative power of love, resilience, and tradition. They offer a window into how the interplay of personal relationships and cultural heritage can forge a path toward artistic greatness. The lessons learned within the intimate confines of home, from the gentle guidance of a nurturing parent to the communal strength of a tightly knit family, have left an indelible mark on a man whose life and work continue to inspire. These early influences remain a crucial part of the mosaic that is Pierce Brosnan—an artist whose depth is as profound as the roots from which he sprang.

Chapter 2: Discovering the Stage.

Journey into Acting

Pierce Brosnan's journey into acting is a story of discovery, determination, and the transformative power of the performing arts. From an early age, Brosnan felt an inexplicable pull toward storytelling, a desire to inhabit characters and breathe life into tales that resonated with audiences. His early years were marked by a growing fascination with drama, nurtured in both informal settings and through early exposure to local theatre and television. This passion would eventually propel him into a career that not only redefined his own identity but also enriched the cinematic landscape with his charismatic presence.

Growing up in Ireland and later transitioning to England, Brosnan experienced a rich blend of cultural influences that nurtured his appreciation for the dramatic arts. In his native Ireland, the power of oral storytelling, steeped in folklore and tradition, left an indelible mark on him. Even as a child, the vibrant legends and poetic narratives of his homeland sparked his imagination. These formative experiences instilled in him an awareness of the beauty and depth of narrative expression—a quality that would later distinguish his performances. In England, a more structured educational environment and exposure to institutional theatre further shaped his understanding of the stage. The opportunity to participate in school plays and local productions provided him with a tangible outlet for his burgeoning talent.

Brosnan's early forays into acting were not the result of a predetermined career path but rather the natural evolution of a young man discovering his voice. Initially, acting was simply one of several creative outlets. However, it soon became clear that his natural affinity for performance set him apart. There was a magnetic quality to the way he embraced roles, whether in small, community-based productions or in early television appearances. Each performance was an exploration—a chance to step into another's skin and explore the complexities of human emotion. It was this fearless approach to character that captured the attention of local directors and mentors, who recognized his raw talent and encouraged him to pursue the craft with a professional commitment.

The turning point in Brosnan's journey was his decision to immerse himself fully in the world of acting. Recognizing that passion alone was not enough, he began to study the intricacies of performance with the seriousness of a scholar. This period was marked by countless hours spent rehearsing, reading scripts, and observing the work of established actors. Brosnan's commitment to the craft was evident in his relentless pursuit of excellence. He sought out every opportunity to learn—from community theatre productions to small television roles—each experience serving as a building block in his evolving technique. This stage of his career was not without its challenges. Like many aspiring actors, he encountered setbacks and moments of doubt. Yet, these challenges only served to fortify his resolve. Each audition, each rejection, was transformed into a learning experience, a necessary step on the long and winding road toward mastery.

During this formative period, Brosnan also began to understand the power of collaboration. Acting is, at its core, a communal art form—one that depends on the interplay between actors, directors, and audiences. Working alongside fellow performers, he learned to appreciate the subtle dynamics of teamwork, improvisation, and shared creative vision. These experiences underscored the importance of trust and vulnerability in the acting process. They taught him that every performance was not just an individual endeavor, but a dialogue—a shared journey toward a common artistic goal. This lesson in collaboration would later prove invaluable as he navigated the complexities of film and stage, where the synergy between cast and crew often makes the difference between an ordinary production and a truly memorable work of art.

Another key aspect of Brosnan's early journey into acting was the evolution of his personal style. Initially influenced by the dramatic traditions of his homeland, he gradually developed a unique approach that blended the emotive expressiveness of Irish storytelling with the refined technique of British theatre. His early roles showcased a balance of passion and restraint—a reflection of his dual heritage. This balance would become one of his most distinguishing characteristics as an actor, setting him apart from his contemporaries and endearing him to audiences around the world.

As Brosnan's experience grew, so did his ambition. The transition from stage to screen was a natural progression, driven by the realization that film offered an even broader canvas on which to express his talents. Early television roles and minor film appearances provided him with invaluable exposure to the different demands of camera work and live performance. Each project was a learning curve, teaching him the nuances of adapting stage techniques for the screen. The intimacy of film required a subtlety of expression—a quiet intensity that could convey meaning without the theatricality often associated with the stage.

Brosnan's ability to modulate his performance to suit different mediums was a testament to his evolving artistry and his relentless drive to hone his craft.

In essence, Pierce Brosnan's journey into acting is emblematic of the transformative potential of the arts. It is a story of a young man who, through perseverance and a deep-seated passion for storytelling, carved out a niche for himself in a competitive field. His early experiences—filled with moments of triumph and challenges—laid the foundation for a career that would see him evolve from a promising newcomer into one of the most respected and beloved figures in the film industry. Brosnan's commitment to continuous learning and his willingness to embrace both the highs and lows of the acting process have left an indelible mark on his work, ensuring that his contributions to film and theatre will be remembered for generations to come.

Training at the Drama Centre London

After embarking on his journey into acting, Pierce Brosnan sought to refine his raw talent by pursuing formal training at the prestigious Drama Centre London. Known for its rigorous curriculum and its focus on method acting, the institution provided Brosnan with an environment in which he could immerse himself fully in the craft. His years at the Drama Centre were transformative, offering him not only technical proficiency but also a deep understanding of the emotional and psychological underpinnings of performance.

The decision to attend Drama Centre London was more than just a step toward professional legitimacy—it was an affirmation of Brosnan's commitment to the art of acting. At the Centre, he encountered a philosophy of performance that emphasized authenticity and vulnerability. The training was famously intense, requiring students to confront not only the external demands of physicality and voice but also the inner workings of their emotional landscape. This holistic approach to acting—blending technical skills with emotional truth—resonated deeply with Brosnan, who had already begun to understand that acting was as much about internal exploration as it was about external expression.

During his time at Drama Centre London, Brosnan was immersed in a curriculum that demanded discipline, focus, and an unwavering commitment to self-improvement. The daily regimen was rigorous: long hours of rehearsals, scene studies, and exercises designed to strip away pretense and reveal the raw core of the performer. Under the guidance of seasoned instructors, he learned to dissect a script with surgical precision, identifying the motivations and inner conflicts of each character. This analytical approach was crucial in developing the layered performances for which he would later become known. Each exercise was an opportunity to experiment with different techniques—from improvisation to method acting—allowing him to explore the full spectrum of his emotional range.

One of the most significant aspects of his training was the emphasis on embracing vulnerability. The instructors at Drama

Centre London believed that true art comes from a place of honesty and openness. Students were encouraged to draw from their own experiences, using personal memories and emotions as a wellspring for their performances. For Brosnan, this meant confronting aspects of his own identity and experiences that had previously been relegated to the background. The process was both cathartic and challenging, as it required a level of introspection that was unfamiliar to him at the time. However, the result was a deepened understanding of his craft—a realization that the power of acting lies in its capacity to reveal universal truths through personal experience.

The physicality of performance was another crucial element of Brosnan's training. The Drama Centre's program was renowned for its focus on body awareness and movement, emphasizing that the body is an instrument of expression. Through a series of physical exercises, dance classes, and movement workshops, Brosnan learned how to harness his body's potential to communicate emotion without words. This training was instrumental in shaping his later performances, where a subtle gesture or a shift in posture often conveyed as much as dialogue. The physical discipline he acquired during these years allowed him to seamlessly transition between the demands of stage and screen, where the nuance of physical expression plays a critical role in storytelling.

Beyond the technical skills, the Drama Centre London experience was a crucible for developing resilience and self-confidence. The competitive nature of the training environment meant that students were constantly pushed to their limits—emotionally, physically, and intellectually. For Brosnan, this was a period of significant personal growth. The challenges he faced in the classroom and on stage forced him to confront his insecurities, to learn from his mistakes, and to build a foundation of confidence that would serve him throughout his career. The rigour of the training instilled in him a strong work ethic and a belief that talent must be continually nurtured and refined—a lesson that would prove invaluable in the unpredictable world of acting.

The camaraderie among students was another noteworthy aspect of his experience at the Drama Centre. Despite the competitive atmosphere, there was a palpable sense of solidarity among those who shared the same passion for acting. Fellow students became both collaborators and critics, offering support and honest feedback that helped refine each other's performances. This collective learning experience fostered a spirit of mutual growth and respect—a microcosm of the broader artistic community. For Brosnan, these relationships were instrumental in shaping his collaborative approach to acting, where every performance is seen as part of a larger creative dialogue.

Reflecting on his time at the Drama Centre London, Brosnan has often cited the institution as a turning point in his career. The lessons learned within its walls went far beyond technical proficiency; they transformed his understanding of what it meant to be an actor. The rigorous training, the emotional breakthroughs, and the deep connections forged during those formative years provided him with the tools to tackle complex characters and challenging roles later in his career. Moreover, the emphasis on authenticity, vulnerability, and continuous self-improvement became guiding principles that have defined his approach to every role he has undertaken.

Pierce Brosnan's years at Drama Centre London were pivotal in sculpting his identity as an actor. The experience was marked by an intense commitment to mastering the craft, a willingness to explore the depths of personal emotion, and the development of both technical and collaborative skills that would serve him well in his professional journey. This period of disciplined training and transformative personal growth not only honed his natural talent but also laid the groundwork for a career characterized by depth, nuance, and a profound understanding of the human condition. The legacy of those years is evident in every performance he delivers—a testament to the enduring power of rigorous artistic training and the relentless pursuit of excellence.

Chapter 3: Breakthrough with Remington Steele

Landing the Titular Role

Pierce Brosnan's journey toward becoming Remington Steele is a story of fortuitous timing, innate charm, and the realization of a creative concept that transformed an unknown actor into a television icon. In the early 1980s, after years of stage work and minor roles on television and film, Brosnan found himself at a crossroads—a moment when a role that perfectly suited his unique blend of magnetism and vulnerability was about to change his life forever.

The concept behind Remington Steele was ingenious: a talented private detective, Laura Holt, frustrated by the prejudice of clients who would not hire a woman, invents an imaginary, suave, male boss to bolster her credibility. Neither she nor the audience expected that a charming and enigmatic con man would step into that role for real. Brosnan was cast as this elusive figure—a man who could seamlessly shift between being a mysterious imposter and an indispensable partner in solving crimes. His casting was not merely luck; it was the culmination of years spent honing his craft and a recognition by the creative team that his screen presence could elevate the character beyond a simple ruse.

At the time, Brosnan was still building his resume. He had studied at the Drama Centre London and worked in various stage productions and small television parts. Yet it was his previous work—his poise on stage, the subtlety of his expressions, and his natural flair for embodying both confidence and sensitivity—that caught the producers' attention. When NBC sought a new series blending detective fiction, romance, and humor, creators Robert Butler and Michael Gleason were determined to cast someone who could carry a character who was at once elusive and compelling. Although originally conceived as a supporting element to Stephanie Zimbalist's Laura Holt, the role was transformed into a lead part thanks to Brosnan's undeniable charisma.

Despite suggestions that the role might have gone to a more traditionally "posh" actor, Brosnan's willingness to embrace the character's duality—channeling the cool detachment of a con man while hinting at a deep-seated vulnerability—won over the decision-makers. His look, marked by rugged Irish features softened by undeniable charm, was exactly what the role needed. Brosnan's portrayal redefined the archetype of the television detective by blending film noir influences with the relaxed, witty sensibility of 1980s TV.

Casting directors recall that during his audition, Brosnan not only demonstrated impeccable timing and a knack for comedic nuance but also captured an enigmatic allure. Every quip and subtle glance conveyed a man who was far more than his outward appearance suggested. Audiences were immediately drawn to his embodiment of Remington Steele, turning an invented persona into a fully realized character. His ability to shift between vulnerability and bravado set the stage for a performance that would become a touchstone of the series.

The decision to cast Brosnan as Remington Steele was a masterstroke. His interpretation was layered with self-awareness, resonating with viewers and marking him as the new face of cool sophistication on television. His portrayal balanced wit with an occasional hint of melancholy, drawing audiences into a narrative that was both entertaining and emotionally engaging. His breakthrough role transformed him from a talented but obscure actor into a household name, laying the groundwork for his future in film.

Moreover, the production environment of Remington Steele nurtured his talent. The collaborative spirit on set, the willingness of the producers to experiment with narrative structure, and the blending of genres all provided Brosnan with the creative freedom to explore the nuances of his character. His on-screen partnership with Stephanie Zimbalist, despite occasional off-camera tensions, became one of the series' defining features and contributed significantly to its success.

In retrospect, landing the titular role in Remington Steele was more than a career-defining moment—it was a turning point that allowed Brosnan to step into the spotlight and shape his future. The role offered him a platform to showcase his talent to a global audience and paved the way for his transition into major film roles, including the iconic portrayal of James Bond. His breakthrough in Remington Steele is a testament to the power of seizing the right opportunity and transforming an offhand concept into a lasting cultural phenomenon.

Impact on His Career Trajectory

The breakthrough role in Remington Steele proved to be a watershed moment for Pierce Brosnan, dramatically altering his career and propelling him into international stardom. Before the series, Brosnan had worked steadily in theater and television but was largely known as a supporting actor. Remington Steele changed that by giving him a platform that showcased his acting prowess and natural screen charisma, transforming him into one of the most recognizable faces on television.

Remington Steele became a cultural phenomenon in the early 1980s, and Brosnan's performance was central to its success. The series—an inventive blend of mystery, romance, and comedy—captured the imagination of audiences, who were drawn to the clever interplay between the determined detective, Laura Holt, and her enigmatic "boss," Remington Steele. For Brosnan, the role was a baptism by fire into the world of mass-market entertainment. His portrayal resonated with viewers because of the unique combination of charm and mystery he brought to the character, qualities that would later define his public persona.

One of the most significant impacts of the role was the vast visibility it provided. With Remington Steele airing on NBC, a network with an extensive reach in the United States and internationally, Brosnan's face became instantly recognizable. This exposure transformed him from a promising young actor into a household name. Casting directors and producers began to see him as not just a skilled performer but as a bankable leading man. His work on the series demonstrated that he could handle a recurring role with depth and nuance—a quality that would later serve him well in major film projects.

The success of Remington Steele opened numerous doors for Brosnan. His performance allowed him to transition seamlessly into film roles that further established his reputation. Projects like The Fourth Protocol (1987) and The Deceivers (1988) benefited from the credibility and audience recognition he had built on television. Critics began to appreciate his ability to convey complex emotions, balancing humor with serious dramatic undertones. This versatility was crucial when he eventually stepped into the role of James Bond—a role that required a similar blend of suaveness, wit, and emotional depth.

Indeed, it was Brosnan's portrayal of Remington Steele that caught the attention of James Bond producers. His ability to embody a character who was both mysterious and disarmingly charming made him an ideal candidate for the role of the world's most famous spy. Although contractual obligations with the series initially complicated his transition, the buzz generated by Remington Steele played a critical role in paving the way for his eventual casting as James Bond in the mid-1990s. His success in the Bond films—GoldenEye, Tomorrow Never Dies, The World Is Not Enough, and Die Another Day—can be traced directly back to the foundation laid during his Remington Steele days.

Beyond opening the door to the Bond franchise, Remington Steele allowed Brosnan to diversify his roles. The character's inherent ambiguity—oscillating between deceit and sincerity—mirrored the complexities of many leading roles in contemporary cinema. This experience taught him how to navigate the fine line between heroism and vulnerability, a skill that would prove invaluable as he took on a wide variety of roles in thrillers, dramas, and comedies. His growing body of work showcased his versatility and helped him develop a signature style characterized by understated elegance and approachability.

Working on Remington Steele also provided Brosnan with a profound understanding of the collaborative nature of television and film production. The long hours and creative challenges of producing a hit series taught him the importance of teamwork and the power of chemistry between co-stars. His on-screen partnership with Stephanie Zimbalist, for example, became one of the defining aspects of the show and demonstrated how dynamic collaborations can elevate a project. This lesson in collaboration influenced his later choices, particularly when working with ensemble casts in major films.

The impact of Remington Steele on Brosnan's career is evident in the way it reshaped industry perceptions. Before the series, he was seen as a talented actor with potential, but after its success, he was recognized as a star. His newfound status allowed him to negotiate higher-profile roles and better contracts, further solidifying his position in Hollywood. In many ways, Remington Steele served as both a launching pad and a proving ground, confirming that Brosnan was ready to take on more challenging and diverse roles.

In summary, the breakthrough provided by Remington Steele was transformative for Pierce Brosnan. It not only elevated his public profile but also refined his acting style, paving the way for his transition into major film roles and ultimately into the iconic world of James Bond. The legacy of Remington Steele remains a testament to the power of a well-conceived role to redefine an actor's career, turning a once-unknown talent into an international star and influencing the trajectory of popular culture for decades to come.

Chapter 4: Personal Triumphs and Tragedies.

Marriage to Cassandra Harris

Pierce Brosnan's personal life took a significant turn when he married Cassandra Harris—a relationship that not only shaped his private world but also had an enduring impact on his professional journey. Their union, formed during a period when Brosnan was emerging as a promising actor, became a defining chapter of his life. It was a marriage marked by shared passions, creative collaboration, and the forging of a bond that would sustain him through the challenges of a demanding career in the entertainment industry.

Cassandra Harris, herself an accomplished actress, brought an undeniable grace and strength to her roles. Meeting on the set of a James Bond film where she appeared as a Bond girl, the couple quickly found common ground in their love for the craft. For Brosnan, Cassandra was more than just a partner—she was a confidante and a muse.

The early days of their relationship were filled with mutual encouragement, as both navigated the uncertainties of a career in show business. Harris's talent and warmth offered Brosnan a glimpse of the kind of stability and creative energy that would later become essential to his development as a star.

Their marriage, which began in the late 1970s, was a beacon of hope during a time when Brosnan was still forging his path in both theater and television. With Cassandra by his side, he found not only emotional support but also an ally who understood the demands and peculiarities of the entertainment world. Their relationship blossomed as they balanced the public's gaze with the private moments of genuine affection and partnership. Harris's presence in Brosnan's life provided a counterbalance to the pressures of constant auditions and the relentless pursuit of roles that could define one's career.

Professionally, the influence of their union became apparent as Brosnan's star began to rise. Harris not only shared her own experiences and insights from the film sets but also served as a subtle force behind the scenes. Her background in acting enriched Brosnan's understanding of character, dialogue, and the delicate interplay of on-screen chemistry. In a sense, their marriage was both a personal and professional collaboration—one that allowed him to draw inspiration from their shared experiences while also learning to navigate the complexities of a high-profile career.

As the couple's relationship deepened, they faced the challenges of balancing a busy professional life with their commitment to each other. For Brosnan, the security of having Cassandra's unwavering support was critical during a period of transition and growth. Whether on set or off, her presence was a steady reminder of the values of loyalty and perseverance. Their home became a sanctuary from the hustle of Hollywood, a place where creative ideas were nurtured, and personal setbacks were met with resilience. In interviews, Brosnan has often recalled the strength he derived from his relationship with Cassandra—how her optimism and gentle encouragement helped him overcome moments of self-doubt and uncertainty.

The marriage also had a profound impact on his public image. Brosnan's transition from a relatively unknown actor to a rising star was accompanied by the media's fascination with his personal life. The couple's relationship was portrayed as one of those rare, enduring partnerships in an industry often characterized by fleeting romances. Cassandra's dignified demeanor and her role as a supportive partner enhanced Brosnan's appeal as both a leading man on screen and a man of substance off screen. It wasn't just his rugged good looks or his suave performances that captivated audiences; it was also the story of a man who found true companionship and, through that, a deeper understanding of himself.

Their union, however, was not without its complexities. Like many relationships formed under the intense scrutiny of Hollywood, there were moments when the demands of their careers threatened to encroach upon their personal time. The constant travel, long shooting schedules, and the unpredictable nature of film and television work meant that time together was often scarce. Yet, it was precisely these challenges that tested and ultimately strengthened their bond. They learned to cherish the rare moments of intimacy and to find solace in the shared understanding of each other's sacrifices. This period of their lives is remembered not for its challenges alone but for the resilience and commitment that saw them through the highs and lows of life in the spotlight.

Tragically, the story of their marriage took a heart-wrenching turn when Cassandra Harris was diagnosed with ovarian cancer—a battle that would eventually claim her life. Even as her illness progressed, the couple's relationship remained a source of strength and inspiration for Brosnan. In the face of her declining health, Harris continued to display remarkable courage and grace, qualities that left an indelible mark on Brosnan's character. Her determination to face the disease head-on, while maintaining a sense of dignity and humor, taught him invaluable lessons about love, loss, and the transient nature of life.

In reflecting on his marriage to Cassandra Harris, Brosnan often speaks of her with deep affection and gratitude. Her influence is evident not only in his personal growth but also in the way he approaches his craft and his public life. She was, and in many ways still is, a guiding light—a reminder of the power of love and the importance of finding strength in one's personal relationships. Their marriage, despite its eventual sorrow, remains a testament to the beauty of genuine connection and the lasting impact one person can have on another's life.

Ultimately, the marriage to Cassandra Harris was a defining period for Pierce Brosnan—a time when he learned the true meaning of partnership and discovered the power of resilience. It was a union that enriched his life, molded his character, and set the stage for the many triumphs and trials that would follow. For Brosnan, Cassandra Harris is remembered not just as a wife and collaborator but as a pivotal influence whose legacy continues to shape his journey as both an actor and a human being.

Navigating Personal Loss and Resilience

Following the profound joy and support of his marriage to Cassandra Harris, Pierce Brosnan's life was later marked by deep personal loss—a series of tragedies that tested his inner strength and ultimately forged a resilient spirit. The painful journey through grief, marked by the loss of his wife and later other family members, is a testament to his ability to navigate life's most challenging moments with dignity, determination, and hope.

The death of Cassandra Harris in 1991 was a pivotal moment in Brosnan's life. Losing a life partner, someone who had been both a personal anchor and a creative collaborator, left a void that seemed impossible to fill. In the midst of a burgeoning career, this personal tragedy forced him to confront the stark reality of mortality. Despite the immense sorrow, Brosnan's response to this loss became a defining chapter in his personal evolution. He has spoken in various interviews about the profound impact that Cassandra's passing had on him—how it reshaped his outlook on life, art, and the fleeting nature of time.

In dealing with the loss of Cassandra, Brosnan embraced both vulnerability and determination. Rather than retreating from the world, he chose to honor her memory by channeling his grief into his work and philanthropic efforts. Her passing spurred him to become actively involved in cancer awareness initiatives, dedicating time and resources to help others facing similar battles. This commitment to advocacy is a reflection of how personal pain can transform into a force for positive change. For Brosnan, supporting cancer research and raising awareness became a way to ensure that Cassandra's legacy would live on—a legacy defined by courage and compassion in the face of overwhelming adversity.

Navigating such profound loss was not a linear journey. It involved periods of deep introspection, moments of self-doubt, and the gradual realization that healing was possible, even if it meant learning to live with the scars. Brosnan's ability to draw strength from his memories of Cassandra and from the love they shared speaks to his resilience. He has often described this process as one of continual growth—a rebuilding of one's self in the wake of tragedy. The emotional lessons learned during this time not only shaped his personal life but also influenced his approach to his craft, infusing his later performances with a depth of emotion that resonated with audiences.

The resilience Brosnan demonstrated in the aftermath of Cassandra's death is mirrored in his handling of subsequent personal losses. In later years, he faced additional heartache, including the loss of his daughter Charlotte—a tragedy that compounded the sorrow already etched into his life. Each loss, while devastating, became part of a larger narrative of survival and personal evolution. Instead of succumbing to despair,

Brosnan used these experiences to deepen his empathy and understanding of the human condition. This emotional maturity is evident in the nuanced performances he delivered in roles that required a sensitivity to pain and an ability to convey complex inner turmoil.

Beyond the realm of his personal relationships, Brosnan's journey through grief also had a significant impact on his public persona. He became known not just as a charismatic leading man on screen but as a person of great emotional depth off screen. His willingness to speak candidly about his experiences with loss and his ongoing efforts to support cancer research and other charitable causes have earned him widespread respect. Audiences and colleagues alike see in him a man who, despite enduring unimaginable sorrow, continues to approach life with a sense of hope and purpose. This resilience has not only defined his personal narrative but also helped shape the legacy he continues to build as an actor and humanitarian.

In many ways, navigating personal loss taught Brosnan the importance of balancing vulnerability with strength. It forced him to confront his innermost fears and insecurities and to emerge on the other side with a greater sense of clarity and commitment. His journey through grief is a reminder that while loss can alter the course of one's life, it does not have to define it. Instead, it can become the impetus for a renewed focus on what truly matters—love, compassion, and the pursuit of a meaningful life.

The impact of these personal tragedies extends into Brosnan's work in film and television as well. The raw emotion that he experienced has enriched his performances, allowing him to convey a spectrum of feelings that resonate deeply with viewers. His characters often embody a quiet strength—a reflection of his own ability to endure hardship and to continue moving forward despite the pain. This authenticity, borne of lived experience, has set him apart as an actor capable of delivering performances that are both captivating and profoundly human.

Ultimately, Pierce Brosnan's journey of navigating personal loss and building resilience is a powerful testament to the human spirit. It is a story of a man who faced heartbreak head-on, chose to honor the memory of those he loved by giving back, and emerged from tragedy with a renewed sense of purpose. His personal triumphs and the sorrow he has endured have coalesced into a legacy defined not only by his cinematic achievements but also by his unwavering commitment to living a life marked by empathy, strength, and hope.

Together, these experiences have molded Brosnan into an individual who is as admired for his personal courage as he is for his on-screen charisma—a man whose journey of loss and resilience continues to inspire those who follow his work and his life.

Chapter 5: Becoming Bond.

The Road to Portraying James Bond

Pierce Brosnan's journey toward becoming James Bond is a fascinating tale of persistence, timing, and transformation—a narrative that saw an actor whose early breakthrough on television with Remington Steele eventually catapult him into one of cinema's most iconic roles. The road to Bond was not a straightforward one; it involved contractual complexities, shifting industry dynamics, and an evolving public image that prepared Brosnan to take on the mantle of 007.

In the mid-1980s, Brosnan's rising star was already evident to many industry insiders. His portrayal of the enigmatic Remington Steele had earned him comparisons to the suave secret agent, with some even suggesting that his natural charm and screen presence made him a perfect candidate to replace Roger Moore as James Bond. In fact, early press reports and interviews noted that "Pierce Brosnan could make it as a young James Bond" – a sentiment that lingered in the minds of producers and casting directors alike.

However, the road to Bond was fraught with obstacles. At the time, Brosnan was under contract to Remington Steele, a popular NBC series that had become a cornerstone of his early career. This commitment meant that when the opportunity to play Bond first emerged—specifically for the film The Living Daylights—Brosnan was unable to accept the role. Instead, the producers turned to Timothy Dalton, who went on to deliver two Bond films in the late 1980s. Brosnan's association with Remington Steele inadvertently blocked his immediate entry into the Bond franchise, despite the fact that many in the industry recognized his potential to bring a fresh and modern interpretation to the role.

The turning point came in the early 1990s, when the Bond series found itself at a crossroads. Following a hiatus due to legal and production complications, the franchise needed a new direction. GoldenEye (1995) emerged as a project that would redefine Bond for a new generation, and Brosnan was finally offered the role. By then, Remington Steele had ended its run, and the gap allowed Brosnan to transition without contractual conflict. The producers, notably Albert R. Broccoli and his successors, saw in Brosnan a blend of the classic Bond charm with a contemporary edge—a combination that had been hinted at during his earlier television work.

Brosnan's casting was not simply the result of his previous successes; it was also a calculated decision by the producers to rejuvenate a franchise that had become somewhat stale in the wake of the earlier Moore and Dalton eras. In many interviews, Brosnan has described the process as both surreal and humbling. The allure of playing Bond lay in the role's rich legacy—a character who was not only a suave secret agent but also a cultural icon. Brosnan's own background, from his Irish roots to his years spent perfecting his craft at the Drama Centre London and on the stage, contributed to a persona that was both worldly and approachable. This made him a compelling choice to bring the character into a modern context.

Industry insiders often recount how Brosnan's performance in GoldenEye was a revelation. His portrayal balanced a sophisticated sense of humor with the stoic determination and physicality required of Bond. Unlike some of his predecessors, Brosnan brought a nuanced vulnerability to the role—a man who was confident and debonair yet capable of revealing his inner struggles and personal losses. His chemistry with co-stars, his crisp delivery of witty one-liners, and his ability to perform demanding action sequences all contributed to a portrayal that resonated with both long-time Bond fans and new audiences.

The road to becoming Bond also involved Brosnan's own inner evolution. Accepting the role meant embracing a character whose legacy was both revered and scrutinized. For Brosnan, stepping into the shoes of James Bond was not merely about donning a tuxedo and delivering catchphrases; it was about capturing the essence of a mythic figure while making it his own. The preparation involved studying previous Bond films, understanding the nuances of Ian Fleming's creation, and finding a balance between paying homage to tradition and pushing the boundaries of what the character could represent in the 1990s and beyond.

Ultimately, the journey was a blend of professional readiness and personal growth. Brosnan's experiences on television and in film had prepared him for the high expectations of the Bond role, and his natural charisma combined with a disciplined approach to acting allowed him to step confidently into one of the most challenging roles in cinema. His casting in GoldenEye marked the beginning of a transformative era—not only for his career but for the Bond franchise itself. With each subsequent film, Brosnan's interpretation would continue to evolve, reflecting the changing tastes of audiences and the dynamic nature of the character.

Brosnan's road to portraying James Bond is a testament to the unpredictable nature of show business—a path that required waiting, perseverance, and the ability to seize the right moment when it finally arrived. It was a journey marked by both setbacks and breakthroughs, where contractual obligations once stood in the way of destiny, only for the stars to align later and propel him into the spotlight as 007. This transformation not only redefined his career but also ensured that his version of Bond would leave an indelible mark on popular culture for years to come.

Analysis of His Performances in GoldenEye, Tomorrow Never Dies, The World Is Not Enough, and Die Another Day

Pierce Brosnan's tenure as James Bond is characterized by a unique blend of charm, sophistication, and a touch of vulnerability that redefined the character for a modern era. Over the course of four films—GoldenEye, Tomorrow Never Dies, The World Is Not Enough, and Die Another Day—Brosnan brought consistency and evolution to the role, each film reflecting shifts in both his interpretation and the broader cultural context. An analysis of these performances reveals how he balanced traditional elements of Bond with contemporary sensibilities, creating a legacy that still resonates with audiences today.

GoldenEye (1995) served as the debut for Brosnan's Bond and set the tone for his interpretation. In this film, Brosnan reintroduced Bond as a character who combined the suave confidence of the classic spy with a renewed physicality and emotional depth. The film itself was a fresh take on the franchise, departing from the campier tone of previous entries and embracing a grittier, more realistic style. Brosnan's performance was marked by a relaxed charisma—he delivered witty one-liners with impeccable timing, exuding an air of effortless cool. His ability to navigate the film's complex action sequences while also engaging in subtle moments of introspection was a clear signal that his Bond was both a man of action and a man with feelings. Critics noted that his portrayal in GoldenEye was a "decided improvement" over his immediate predecessor, as he managed to capture both the charm and the occasional vulnerability of Bond.

In Tomorrow Never Dies (1997), Brosnan's Bond faced a media-savvy adversary, reflecting the growing influence of technology and information warfare in the late 1990s. Here, Brosnan's performance had to balance physicality with an intellectual coolness—a Bond who was not only a skilled fighter but also a master of strategic maneuvering in a world where information was power. His delivery in key scenes was measured and deliberate, suggesting a deep understanding of the character's internal conflicts. The film's narrative allowed Brosnan to explore Bond's personal side more explicitly, as moments of quiet reflection contrasted sharply with the high-octane action sequences. His portrayal was praised for its subtlety; even in the face of explosive set pieces, there was a calm assurance in his performance that reassured the audience that Bond was always in control.

The World Is Not Enough (1999) further expanded Brosnan's interpretation of Bond by delving into themes of loyalty, betrayal, and the personal costs of a life in espionage. This film presented Bond as a more complex character—one who was grappling with personal loss while being drawn into a plot that blurred the lines between duty and emotion. Brosnan's performance in this installment was imbued with a sense of melancholy that hinted at the burdens of his secretive life. He allowed the audience to see a Bond who was more reflective, capable of experiencing deep emotional conflict even as he executed his missions with precision. This nuanced approach added layers to the character and demonstrated Brosnan's willingness to evolve Bond beyond a mere action hero. His interactions with co-stars and his measured delivery of poignant dialogue underscored a more introspective side of Bond, one that resonated with viewers who had grown accustomed to a more humanized spy.

Die Another Day (2002) marked the final chapter of Brosnan's tenure as Bond, and it is perhaps the most polarizing of his films. While the film embraced a modern, high-tech aesthetic and featured bold set pieces—including the infamous ice palace and a high-octane car chase—the performance of Bond under Brosnan's portrayal continued to carry his signature charm. Despite criticisms of the film's overblown elements and reliance on CGI, Brosnan's Bond remained a bastion of cool under pressure. His performance here is notable for its unwavering consistency; even amidst the film's more fantastical aspects, Brosnan delivered lines and scenes with the same effortless sophistication he had established in GoldenEye. In Die Another Day, Bond's character is both larger than life and deeply human—a combination that Brosnan managed to convey through subtle gestures, understated humor, and a resilient presence that hinted at the trials of his past films. Although opinions on the film were divided, many critics agreed that Brosnan's portrayal was a strong final note on his interpretation of Bond—a fitting capstone that balanced the character's mythic stature with the vulnerabilities that had been introduced in previous films.

Across these four films, Brosnan's performance as Bond can be seen as a carefully calibrated evolution. In GoldenEye, he established the foundation with a blend of wit, charm, and understated toughness.

Tomorrow Never Dies built on this by introducing more cerebral and introspective moments, reflecting the shifting landscape of global politics and technology. The World Is Not Enough added a layer of emotional complexity that hinted at the personal costs of Bond's lifestyle, while Die Another Day, despite its extravagance, maintained the core elements of his established persona. Throughout these films, Brosnan consistently managed to bring a sense of continuity to the character while also allowing him to evolve with the times.

Critics and fans alike have noted that Brosnan's Bond is characterized by an inherent balance—a man who is as comfortable in a tuxedo delivering a razor-sharp quip as he is in the midst of an adrenaline-fueled action sequence. His physical presence, combined with a refined manner of speech and a measured approach to danger, created a version of Bond that felt both timeless and contemporary. The humor in his performance, often delivered with a knowing smile or a subtle raised eyebrow, added a layer of sophistication that distinguished his Bond from the more bombastic interpretations of the past.

Ultimately, the legacy of Brosnan's portrayal of James Bond is one of reinvention. He took a character steeped in tradition and reimagined him for a new era, balancing modern sensibilities with the enduring appeal of a classic icon. His performances not only reinvigorated the Bond franchise but also set a standard for future interpretations of the character. Brosnan's Bond remains one of the most beloved iterations, appreciated for its mix of elegance, resilience, and a touch of melancholy—a Bond who, despite the high stakes of his world, never lost his cool.

Together, these four films illustrate how Brosnan transformed James Bond into a multifaceted character—a blend of action hero, witty bon vivant, and a man burdened by the weight of his own secrets.

His journey as Bond is a testament to his skill as an actor and his ability to navigate the shifting demands of a franchise while staying true to the essence of a character that continues to capture the imagination of audiences around the world.

Chapter 6: Beyond 007

Diversifying Roles: The Thomas Crown Affair and Dante's Peak

Pierce Brosnan's career after becoming synonymous with James Bond is a testament to his desire to break free from a single, iconic image. Rather than remaining pigeonholed as the suave secret agent, Brosnan deliberately sought roles that allowed him to explore vastly different characters and cinematic worlds. Two of the most notable examples are his performances in The Thomas Crown Affair and Dante's Peak, which not only showcased his versatility but also demonstrated his willingness to take on complex, diverse roles.

In The Thomas Crown Affair, Brosnan steps into the shoes of a sophisticated, enigmatic art thief who leads a double life. This role required him to portray a man who is both intelligent and charming, someone who operates on the fringes of legality with a cool detachment and refined taste. Unlike the world of espionage that he dominated as Bond, Thomas Crown was a character who reveled in high society, art, and the thrill of the heist. Brosnan's performance was characterized by a quiet confidence and an understated allure. He played the role with a measured elegance, where every glance and gesture was loaded with subtext. The cat-and-mouse game between Crown and the insurance investigator, which was central to the film's narrative, allowed Brosnan to demonstrate a more playful, yet calculated side of his acting. His ability to shift seamlessly between moments of intense focus and moments of light-hearted mischief marked a departure from the physicality and high-octane action sequences associated with Bond. Instead, The Thomas Crown Affair demanded subtlety and nuance—a challenge that Brosnan met with aplomb.

On the other end of the spectrum lies Dante's Peak, a disaster film in which Brosnan played a volcanologist thrust into the chaos of an erupting volcano. Here, he was required to adopt an entirely different persona—a scientist whose rational mind battles against the unpredictable forces of nature. In Dante's Peak, Brosnan's character is one of intellect and expertise, tasked with understanding and mitigating a catastrophic natural disaster. This role was a stark contrast to the suave, gentleman thief of The Thomas Crown Affair. In Dante's Peak, the stakes were literal and visceral, and Brosnan's performance needed to convey urgency, tension, and vulnerability. The transformation was evident in the physicality of the role; his character's interactions with the environment, the dramatic pauses in the face of overwhelming natural power, and the emotional weight of facing potential disaster showcased a different range of his abilities. The challenges of filming in demanding, sometimes hazardous conditions also added authenticity to his portrayal, reinforcing his reputation as an actor willing to push his limits in service of the story.

Both films represent distinct ends of the cinematic spectrum—one steeped in the elegance of high art and subtle deception, the other grounded in the raw, unpredictable power of nature. Yet, Brosnan managed to bring a consistent presence to both roles. In each case, his performance was marked by a commitment to authenticity and a refusal to be confined by typecasting. His portrayal of Thomas Crown emphasized a refined intelligence and a sense of daring charm, while his work in Dante's Peak highlighted a more measured, intellectual vulnerability. These roles allowed him to demonstrate that he was more than just Bond; he was a versatile actor capable of delving into characters that required both emotional and physical transformation.

Moreover, diversifying his roles helped Brosnan to reshape his public image. Audiences began to see him as an actor with a broad repertoire, someone who could inhabit a wide array of characters with credibility and nuance. This transition was crucial at a time when the entertainment industry was evolving rapidly, and actors were increasingly expected to be multifaceted. By embracing projects that were so different in tone and style, Brosnan not only expanded his artistic horizons but also ensured that his career would be defined by a rich variety of roles rather than a single character archetype.

Critically, the reception of these films reinforced Brosnan's reputation as a dynamic performer. The Thomas Crown Affair, with its stylish direction and clever narrative, was praised for its fresh take on the heist genre, and Brosnan's role was seen as a refreshing departure from his previous work. Similarly, Dante's Peak was recognized for its ambitious blend of scientific inquiry and disaster-driven drama, with Brosnan's portrayal of the determined volcanologist earning acclaim for its emotional depth and resilience. Both films contributed to a growing body of work that underscored his adaptability and willingness to take risks.

In reflecting on these projects, it becomes clear that Brosnan's decision to diversify was not merely about escaping the confines of his Bond persona. It was an artistic choice aimed at exploring the full spectrum of his abilities, from the subtle intricacies of a high-society con man to the raw, human struggle against nature's fury. By taking on such varied roles, he not only broadened his acting range but also deepened the layers of his professional identity. His journey through these roles illustrates a deliberate, thoughtful process of self-reinvention—one that has allowed him to remain relevant and compelling in a constantly changing industry.

Ultimately, The Thomas Crown Affair and Dante's Peak stand as pivotal examples of how Pierce Brosnan successfully diversified his career. These films are milestones that demonstrate his capacity to adapt and excel in radically different genres, thereby setting the stage for a long and varied career that extends far beyond the confines of a single franchise. They encapsulate the essence of his artistic evolution—a journey marked by bold choices, creative risk-taking, and a relentless pursuit of roles that challenge him to grow as an actor.

Exploring His Range in Different Genres

While Pierce Brosnan's tenure as James Bond remains a cornerstone of his career, his willingness to explore roles in diverse genres has been equally instrumental in defining his artistic identity. Beyond the world of espionage, Brosnan has dipped his toes into a wide variety of cinematic landscapes—from romantic comedies and action thrillers to disaster films and quirky science fiction. This breadth of experience not only showcases his versatility as an actor but also reflects a career-long commitment to challenging himself and reinventing his on-screen persona.

One of the early indicators of Brosnan's range was his role in the family comedy Mrs. Doubtfire (1993), where he played a supporting character in a film that blended humor with poignant family dynamics. Although not the lead, his performance contributed to a film that remains beloved by audiences for its heartwarming narrative and clever humor. This foray into comedy demonstrated that Brosnan was not confined to the cool, calculated world of action and suspense; he could also deliver a performance that resonated on a lighter, more human level.

In contrast, his role in Mars Attacks! (1996), a Tim Burton-directed science fiction comedy, allowed him to explore a more eccentric and playful side. The film, known for its satirical take on alien invasion and the absurdities of modern society, required Brosnan to adopt a persona that was both over-the-top and self-aware. His performance in Mars Attacks! was a clear departure from the stoic Bond archetype. Instead, he embraced the film's surreal humor, delivering his lines with a wry sense of irony that fit perfectly within Burton's whimsical vision. This role underscored his ability to shift gears effortlessly, moving from intense dramatic roles to more fantastical, comedic ones.

Another notable aspect of Brosnan's career is his venture into musical territory with Mamma Mia! (2008) and its sequel, Mamma Mia! Here We Go Again (2018). In these films, Brosnan took on the role of Sam Carmichael, one of the three potential fathers of the lead character, in a project that combined romance, comedy, and musical elements. Although his performance in Mamma Mia! received mixed reviews—and even earned him a Golden Raspberry Award for Worst Supporting Actor—it was a bold choice that exemplified his willingness to experiment. Singing and dancing on screen required a different kind of energy and physicality than his previous roles, and while the film's campy nature may not have suited everyone's taste, it added another layer to his multifaceted career.

Brosnan's ventures into dramatic roles further highlight his range. In films such as The Ghost Writer (2010), directed by Roman Polanski, he delivered a performance that was marked by subtlety and introspection. The film, a political thriller steeped in mystery and tension, required Brosnan to convey an inner turmoil that belied his otherwise polished exterior. His nuanced portrayal of a man caught in a web of political intrigue and personal conflict was a testament to his ability to bring depth and complexity to his characters—an ability that goes far beyond the surface-level charm of his earlier roles.

Moreover, Brosnan's work in disaster films like Dante's Peak, already discussed for its demanding physicality and emotional intensity, further illustrates his capacity to engage with high-stakes narratives. Disaster films require a careful balance between technical expertise and emotional resonance, and Brosnan's performance in Dante's Peak demonstrated that he could handle both with equal finesse. His portrayal of a dedicated scientist grappling with nature's fury showcased not only his physical endurance but also his ability to project vulnerability and resilience in the face of overwhelming odds.

Throughout his career, Brosnan has also taken on roles in smaller, independent films that allow for even greater experimentation. These projects, often characterized by their unique storytelling styles and offbeat characters, have provided him with opportunities to explore themes and narratives that differ significantly from blockbuster fare. In these films, he is free to take risks and inhabit characters that might be too unconventional for mainstream audiences. This willingness to work on diverse projects reflects a deep-seated passion for the craft of acting—one that values artistic exploration over commercial guarantees.

The cumulative effect of these varied roles is a career that defies easy categorization. Brosnan's filmography is a mosaic of genres and styles, each piece contributing to a larger picture of an actor who is unafraid to reinvent himself. Whether he is playing a charming con man, a quirky alien-fighting hero, a sensitive political figure, or a lighthearted romantic lead, Brosnan brings a consistent blend of dedication, nuance, and a distinct personal style to every role.

Critics have often lauded his ability to imbue even the most seemingly superficial roles with a sense of authenticity and gravitas. His performances have a natural quality that suggests a deep understanding of human emotions—a trait that allows him to transition smoothly between genres. This adaptability is one of his greatest strengths and is a major reason why he has remained a relevant and admired figure in an industry that is constantly evolving.

In conclusion, Pierce Brosnan's exploration of different genres is a vivid demonstration of his versatility as an actor. By taking on a broad spectrum of roles—from family comedies and quirky science fiction to intense dramas and disaster films—he has proven that he is not confined to any single image or archetype. His career beyond 007 is marked by a fearless willingness to experiment and to push the boundaries of what is expected, ultimately creating a legacy defined by both breadth and depth. This rich tapestry of roles not only cements his status as one of Hollywood's most adaptable leading men but also serves as an enduring inspiration to actors who strive to break free from typecasting and explore the full range of their abilities.

Pierce Brosnan's life beyond the silver screen is marked by deep familial bonds and a steadfast commitment to environmental advocacy. His personal experiences have profoundly influenced his philanthropic endeavors, painting a portrait of a man dedicated to both his loved ones and the planet.

Family Life with Keely Shaye Smith and Children, Brosnan's journey into family life began with his marriage to Australian actress Cassandra Harris in 1980. Together, they had a son, Sean, and Brosnan adopted Harris's two children, Charlotte and Christopher, from her previous marriage after their father's passing. Tragically, Harris succumbed to ovarian cancer in 1991, a loss that deeply affected Brosnan. Further sorrow struck when Charlotte also died from the same disease in 2013.

In 1994, Brosnan met American journalist Keely Shaye Smith in Mexico. Their relationship blossomed, leading to their marriage in 2001 at Ballintubber Abbey in Ireland. The couple has two sons: Dylan Thomas Brosnan, born on January 13, 1997, and Paris Beckett Brosnan, born on February 27, 2001. Dylan has pursued careers in modeling and music, while Paris has made a name for himself as a model and filmmaker. The Brosnan family primarily resides in Malibu, California, with additional homes in Hawaii and Ireland.

Environmental Activism and Philanthropic Endeavors Beyond his cinematic achievements, Brosnan, alongside Keely Shaye Smith, has been a passionate advocate for environmental causes. The couple co-produced the documentary "Poisoning Paradise," which exposes the environmental and health impacts of pesticide use in Hawaii. Their activism extends to collaborations with organizations like the Natural Resources Defense Council (NRDC), focusing on marine mammal protection and opposing projects detrimental to ocean habitats. Notably, they campaigned against the proposed Cabrillo Port Liquefied Natural Gas facility off the Malibu coast, highlighting potential environmental risks.

Brosnan's philanthropic reach encompasses support for over forty charities addressing diverse causes, including women's healthcare and children's issues. He serves as an International Ambassador for UNICEF, contributing to campaigns like "Unite for Children – Unite Against AIDS." Demonstrating a commitment to education, Brosnan and Smith used proceeds from their wedding coverage to fund the construction of a school in Tibet, providing children with practical skills and knowledge.

In recent years, Brosnan and his son Paris collaborated with the Basel, Rotterdam, and Stockholm Conventions to raise awareness about plastic waste management, emphasizing the importance of addressing global plastic pollution. This initiative underscores the family's dedication to environmental stewardship and intergenerational activism.

Through his personal experiences and public endeavors, Pierce Brosnan exemplifies a life dedicated to family and the betterment of the world, seamlessly integrating his roles as a father, husband, actor, and activist.

Chapter 7: Personal Life and Advocacy

Pierce Brosnan's life beyond the silver screen is marked by deep familial bonds and a steadfast commitment to environmental advocacy. His personal experiences have profoundly influenced his philanthropic endeavors, painting a portrait of a man dedicated to both his loved ones and the planet.

Family Life with Keely Shaye Smith and Children

Brosnan's journey into family life began with his marriage to Australian actress Cassandra Harris in 1980. Together, they had a son, Sean, and Brosnan adopted Harris's two children, Charlotte and Christopher, from her previous marriage after their father's passing. Tragically, Harris succumbed to ovarian cancer in 1991, a loss that deeply affected Brosnan. Further sorrow struck when Charlotte also died from the same disease in 2013.

In 1994, Brosnan met American journalist Keely Shaye Smith in Mexico. Their relationship blossomed, leading to their marriage in 2001 at Ballintubber Abbey in Ireland. The couple has two sons: Dylan Thomas Brosnan, born on January 13, 1997, and Paris Beckett Brosnan, born on February 27, 2001. Dylan has pursued careers in modeling and music, while Paris has made a name for himself as a model and filmmaker. The Brosnan family primarily resides in Malibu, California, with additional homes in Hawaii and Ireland.

Environmental Activism and Philanthropic Endeavors

Beyond his cinematic achievements, Brosnan, alongside Keely Shaye Smith, has been a passionate advocate for environmental causes. The couple co-produced the documentary "Poisoning Paradise," which exposes the environmental and health impacts of pesticide use in Hawaii. Their activism extends to collaborations with organizations like the Natural Resources Defense Council (NRDC), focusing on marine mammal protection and opposing projects detrimental to ocean habitats. Notably, they campaigned against the proposed Cabrillo Port Liquefied Natural Gas facility off the Malibu coast, highlighting potential environmental risks.

Brosnan's philanthropic reach encompasses support for over forty charities addressing diverse causes, including women's healthcare and children's issues. He serves as an International Ambassador for UNICEF, contributing to campaigns like "Unite for Children – Unite Against AIDS." Demonstrating a commitment to education, Brosnan and Smith used proceeds from their wedding coverage to fund the construction of a school in Tibet, providing children with practical skills and knowledge.

In recent years, Brosnan and his son Paris collaborated with the Basel, Rotterdam, and Stockholm Conventions to raise awareness about plastic waste management, emphasizing the importance of addressing global plastic pollution. This initiative underscores the family's dedication to environmental stewardship and intergenerational activism.

Through his personal experiences and public endeavors, Pierce Brosnan exemplifies a life dedicated to family and the betterment of the world, seamlessly integrating his roles as a father, husband, actor, and activist.

Chapter 8: Later Career and Recent Works

Roles in Mamma Mia!, The Matador, and Black Adam

In the later stages of his career, Pierce Brosnan made a deliberate choice to challenge the notion that he was defined solely by his iconic portrayal of James Bond. His diverse filmography from this period reflects a willingness to explore roles that range from musical romantic comedies to dark, offbeat thrillers and even to the realm of superhero blockbusters. Notably, Brosnan's performances in Mamma Mia!, The Matador, and Black Adam illustrate his multifaceted talent and his continuous evolution as an actor.

In 2008, Brosnan appeared in Mamma Mia!, a film adaptation of the hit musical based on the songs of ABBA. In this light-hearted, sun-soaked musical comedy, Brosnan took on the role of Sam Carmichael, one of three men believed to be the potential father of the film's lead character. Although his performance in Mamma Mia! was met with mixed reviews—and even earned him a Golden Raspberry Award for Worst Supporting Actor—it is important to understand the context in which this role was chosen. Brosnan's casting in the film was a bold move, representing his willingness to step into a part that required not only acting but also singing and a different type of physicality. Mamma Mia! allowed him to showcase a more playful, self-aware side of his personality—a stark contrast to the intense, action-packed image he had built as Bond. His portrayal was characterized by a refined charm and a subtle humor that, despite the film's campy nature, endeared him to audiences looking for a lighthearted escape. The film's global success and its enduring popularity on home video and streaming platforms further underscore Brosnan's ability to connect with a broad demographic—even when taking on roles that depart from his previous dramatic intensity.

A few years earlier, in 2005, Brosnan starred in The Matador—a dark comedy that further expanded the boundaries of his on-screen persona. In The Matador, he played Julian Noble, a disillusioned hitman who unexpectedly forms an unlikely friendship with a down-on-his-luck salesman. This role was a significant departure from the traditional suave spy and romantic lead that audiences had come to expect from Brosnan. Instead, The Matador offered him a character layered with cynicism, vulnerability, and a wry sense of humor. Critics praised his performance as one of the best in his career, noting how he managed to blend the deadpan delivery of a hardened assassin with moments of unexpected tenderness. The film's darkly comedic tone and offbeat narrative allowed Brosnan to experiment with irony and self-reflection. He was not merely rehashing the Bond formula; rather, he was recontextualizing his star image in a way that was both daring and refreshingly original. The role in The Matador provided him with an opportunity to break free from the confines of typecasting, proving that he could lead a film that was as unconventional as it was entertaining.

Then, in 2022, Brosnan joined the superhero genre with his role in Black Adam. Portraying the character of Kent Nelson/Doctor Fate in this DC Extended Universe film, Brosnan embraced a role that was steeped in mythology and gravitas. Black Adam, a film known for its larger-than-life action sequences and visually striking set pieces, required Brosnan to adopt a more mature, commanding presence. In this role, he balanced the mystical aspects of Doctor Fate—a figure steeped in ancient lore and magic—with the practical demands of a modern superhero narrative. His portrayal was a study in subtle authority: even when his screen time was limited, Brosnan's every gesture and measured line delivery conveyed the weight of decades of experience and wisdom. His performance in Black Adam was a testament to his ability to transform himself for the demands of a franchise that appeals to a new generation of comic book fans while still honoring the mythic traditions of the source material.

What ties these three roles together is Brosnan's fearless approach to reinvention. In Mamma Mia!, he traded in the tailored tuxedo of a secret agent for a more relaxed, sun-kissed demeanor that played to his natural charm and ease. In The Matador, he adopted a darker, more introspective edge—one that allowed him to explore the complexities of loneliness and disillusionment while still delivering moments of dark humor. And in Black Adam, he stepped into the world of high-stakes superhero narratives, where his gravitas and subtle authority were essential in grounding a fantastical story. In each instance, Brosnan demonstrated that he was not content to rest on the laurels of his past successes. Instead, he continuously sought roles that would challenge his range and allow him to evolve as an actor.

Critically, these performances have played an important role in reshaping public perception of Brosnan. While his work as James Bond remains iconic, his choices in later projects have shown that he is more than just a suave spy. His willingness to tackle varied genres—from musicals to dark comedies to superhero epics—illustrates a commitment to artistic exploration that few actors can claim. Even when faced with projects that did not resonate perfectly with every critic, Brosnan's underlying dedication to his craft shone through. Each role contributed to a broader narrative: that of an actor unafraid to take risks and redefine himself in an ever-changing cinematic landscape.

Moreover, these films allowed Brosnan to expand his fan base. Mamma Mia! reached family audiences and international markets in a way that few films could, while The Matador appealed to fans of offbeat, independent cinema. Black Adam, on the other hand, positioned him within the booming superhero genre—a market that continues to grow and attract diverse audiences worldwide. Through these roles, Brosnan not only maintained relevance in a competitive industry but also demonstrated that his star power could transcend traditional boundaries.

Ultimately, Brosnan's roles in Mamma Mia!, The Matador, and Black Adam serve as landmark achievements in a career defined by versatility. They reveal an actor who is willing to defy expectations and reinvent himself, proving that even after decades in the spotlight, there remains an endless appetite for creative risk-taking. By embracing roles that span a wide spectrum of genres, Brosnan has left an indelible mark on modern cinema—one that speaks to his enduring ability to captivate audiences, adapt to new trends, and continually redefine what it means to be a leading man.

Continued Presence in the Entertainment Industry

Even as the years have passed since his early breakthroughs and iconic roles, Pierce Brosnan's presence in the entertainment industry remains both significant and dynamic. His continued involvement spans film, television, and even stage appearances—each endeavor underscoring a commitment to evolving as an actor and staying relevant in a rapidly changing cultural landscape.

One of the hallmarks of Brosnan's enduring career is his ability to adapt to new trends and technologies while maintaining a distinctive screen presence. Whether it is through high-budget blockbusters or smaller, independent projects, he has consistently sought out roles that challenge him and allow him to grow artistically. This adaptability is evident in his seamless transition from television star to global film icon—a journey that began with Remington Steele and culminated in his celebrated tenure as James Bond. Even after leaving the Bond franchise, Brosnan has managed to cultivate a diverse filmography that resonates with both long-time fans and new audiences.

Brosnan's continued presence is reflected in his willingness to take on projects that diverge from conventional mainstream cinema. For instance, he has appeared in independent films that allow for deeper character exploration, offering him the opportunity to engage in roles that demand subtlety and introspection. These projects not only reinforce his reputation as a versatile actor but also serve as a counterbalance to the commercial pressures of Hollywood. By choosing roles that might be considered unconventional or even risky, Brosnan demonstrates a deep commitment to the craft of acting—a commitment that has kept him relevant well into his later years.

Moreover, Brosnan has embraced the opportunities presented by emerging digital platforms and streaming services. In today's entertainment landscape, where audiences increasingly consume content online, his participation in various streaming projects has ensured that he remains visible and accessible to a younger generation. Whether through guest appearances on popular streaming series, cameo roles, or participation in high-profile digital campaigns, Brosnan has adeptly navigated the evolving industry. This strategic embrace of new media has allowed him to maintain his status as a contemporary actor while also honoring the legacy of his earlier work.

In addition to his film and television work, Brosnan's engagement in other creative ventures further cements his continued presence in the industry. His return to the stage—whether through theatrical productions or live events—has provided audiences with yet another dimension of his talent. These appearances serve as a reminder that his roots in theater remain an integral part of who he is as an actor, and they allow him to connect with audiences in an intimate and immediate way. Furthermore, his ventures into production through his company Irish DreamTime have given him a voice behind the scenes, enabling him to influence the types of projects that get made and ensuring that his creative vision continues to resonate.

Brosnan's longevity is also attributable to his ability to reinvent his public persona without losing the core elements that made him a beloved figure in the first place. He has consistently balanced the image of the charming, debonair leading man with that of a thoughtful, introspective individual. This duality is not only a reflection of his versatility as an actor but also of his personal growth over the decades. Whether he is participating in a blockbuster action film, an indie drama, or a light-hearted romantic comedy, Brosnan brings an authenticity and warmth to his roles that transcend generational boundaries.

Critically, his sustained relevance has not gone unnoticed. Industry insiders, fellow actors, and critics alike continue to laud his contributions to cinema and television. His willingness to discuss his experiences openly—whether in interviews, documentaries, or public appearances—has helped humanize the larger-than-life persona often associated with leading men. Brosnan's thoughtful reflections on his career and his candid discussions about the challenges and triumphs of working in Hollywood resonate with audiences and serve as an inspiration to aspiring actors. His status as both a veteran and an innovator positions him as a bridge between the golden eras of cinema and the new age of digital entertainment.

Furthermore, Brosnan's philanthropic endeavors and advocacy work, particularly in environmental activism and charitable causes, have also contributed to his continued presence in the public eye. By using his platform to champion important social and environmental issues, he has cultivated a reputation as an actor who cares deeply about the world beyond the film set. This commitment not only endears him to fans but also highlights a broader understanding of the responsibilities that come with fame. His efforts in raising awareness about environmental sustainability and supporting various charitable initiatives are a testament to the multifaceted nature of his public persona.

In essence, Pierce Brosnan's ongoing career is a study in resilience and reinvention. From blockbuster films and indie projects to digital streaming ventures and live theater, he has consistently adapted to the evolving demands of the entertainment industry. His ability to remain relevant—a feat achieved by many but mastered by few—stems from his relentless pursuit of roles that challenge him, his embrace of new media, and his unwavering commitment to the craft of acting.

Ultimately, Brosnan's continued presence in the industry is not just a testament to his talent as an actor; it is also a reflection of his willingness to evolve, experiment, and engage with audiences in new and meaningful ways. As the landscape of entertainment continues to shift, Pierce Brosnan remains a constant—a versatile, passionate, and ever-adaptable figure whose career serves as an enduring inspiration to both industry professionals and fans alike.

Chapter 9: Legacy and Influence.

Impact on Cinema and Future Actors

Over the decades, Pierce Brosnan has left an indelible mark on cinema—a legacy that extends far beyond his iconic roles. His work has not only redefined the archetype of the suave leading man but has also inspired a generation of actors to explore a more multifaceted approach to performance. Brosnan's career, spanning stage, television, and film, is a master class in versatility and reinvention, and its influence is evident in how modern cinema approaches character depth, genre-blending, and star power.

Brosnan first captured global attention with his breakthrough role in Remington Steele. Even before he donned the tuxedo as James Bond, his ability to combine charm with an underlying vulnerability set him apart. This blend of qualities has become a benchmark for many actors who seek to balance physical appeal with emotional authenticity. By rejecting the one-dimensional "action hero" mold, Brosnan helped usher in an era where leading men are expected to be both dashing and complex. His nuanced performances encouraged casting directors and filmmakers to look beyond superficial charisma, considering instead an actor's ability to convey layered emotions. In doing so, he contributed to a shift in Hollywood that paved the way for more character-driven narratives.

The impact of Brosnan's approach is perhaps most evident in the evolution of the James Bond franchise itself. When Brosnan took on the role of 007 in GoldenEye, he revitalized the character for a new generation. His Bond was confident yet not impervious to emotion, suave but occasionally introspective. This interpretation resonated with audiences and critics alike, setting a high standard for future Bonds. Brosnan's blend of wit, sophistication, and subtle vulnerability redefined what audiences expected from a secret agent. His influence can be seen in the work of later actors who have been cast in the role—each striving to balance traditional Bond cool with a modern, more human touch.

Beyond Bond, Brosnan's choices in roles have also demonstrated an unwavering commitment to artistic diversity. In films like The Thomas Crown Affair and Dante's Peak, he showcased his ability to embody characters who exist on the fringes of convention. These roles, markedly different from the glamorous world of Bond, underscored his belief that an actor must continuously reinvent himself. In doing so, he became a role model for actors who aspire to break free from typecasting. Many emerging performers cite Brosnan's career as an inspiration, noting how his willingness to take on unconventional roles encouraged them to pursue projects that challenge the status quo. His career trajectory illustrates that longevity in the entertainment industry comes from an artist's readiness to explore new territory and to let go of a single identity.

Brosnan's influence also extends to the broader cinematic landscape. His performances have contributed to the international appeal of Hollywood films, helping to bridge the gap between European sensibilities and American blockbuster styles. As an Irish actor who achieved global fame, he became a symbol of cross-cultural success—a reminder that talent is universal and that great acting transcends borders. His international background and the way he effortlessly shifted between accents and cultural contexts have inspired a new wave of actors to embrace their own heritage as a strength rather than a limitation.

Moreover, Brosnan's off-screen endeavors have further cemented his legacy in the entertainment industry. His involvement in film production through his company Irish DreamTime has given him a hand in shaping the stories that reach audiences. This behind-the-scenes work, often overshadowed by his on-screen achievements, speaks to his commitment to nurturing creative talent and to fostering projects that might not otherwise see the light of day. By mentoring emerging filmmakers and supporting independent projects, Brosnan has contributed to the growth of a diverse and dynamic film community. His efforts have ensured that his influence extends beyond his personal filmography, inspiring future generations of actors and directors to think boldly and creatively.

In addition, Brosnan's candid discussions about the challenges and rewards of his long career have had an educational impact on aspiring performers. In numerous interviews and public appearances, he has shared insights into the realities of working in a highly competitive industry. From negotiating contracts to navigating the pressures of public expectation, his reflections serve as a guide for those entering the field. Future actors benefit not only from his performances but also from his willingness to offer wisdom gained over decades in an industry that is as unpredictable as it is glamorous.

Ultimately, the legacy of Pierce Brosnan's impact on cinema is measured not only in box office numbers or iconic roles but in the way he has redefined the art of acting. His career has challenged future actors to embrace complexity, to seek out roles that push boundaries, and to remain true to their own creative vision. As the industry continues to evolve with new technologies and storytelling methods, Brosnan's influence endures—a reminder that genuine talent and a commitment to artistic exploration remain the cornerstones of great cinema.

In this way, Brosnan has helped to shape the modern landscape of film, setting an example for future actors who aspire to longevity and versatility in their careers. His contributions to character development, genre blending, and international cinematic appeal have left an enduring legacy that will continue to inspire actors and filmmakers for generations to come.

Reflections on a Storied Career

As Pierce Brosnan's career enters its later chapters, reflections on his storied journey evoke both admiration and a deep understanding of what it means to be an artist in a constantly evolving industry. With a career spanning nearly five decades, Brosnan's path from a promising young actor on the stage to a global film icon has been marked by both dazzling triumphs and poignant challenges. His experiences offer rich insights into the nature of fame, the pressures of Hollywood, and the transformative power of resilience.

Brosnan's early breakthrough on television with Remington Steele set the stage for his eventual ascension to the role of James Bond—a role that would define an era of cinema. Yet, even as he embraced the suave, sophisticated persona of 007, he never allowed himself to be confined by that identity. Instead, he continually sought out roles that pushed him to explore new facets of his craft. Reflecting on this journey, Brosnan has often spoken about the importance of reinvention. For him, every role was an opportunity to rediscover himself, to shed one layer of public expectation and to reveal something more authentic and vulnerable. This willingness to evolve has become a hallmark of his career, earning him respect not just for his on-screen performances but also for his courage in taking creative risks.

Throughout his career, Brosnan has weathered both critical and personal storms, emerging each time with a renewed sense of purpose. The highs of becoming Bond and the global recognition that followed were tempered by the personal tragedies that marked his life, including the loss of his first wife, Cassandra Harris, and later, his daughter Charlotte. These experiences, though profoundly painful, have also contributed to the depth and nuance that Brosnan brings to his performances. His personal journey is one of transformation—a story of overcoming adversity and learning to channel grief and loss into creative expression. In interviews, he has acknowledged that these hardships have enriched his understanding of human emotion, enabling him to portray characters with genuine empathy and subtle complexity.

The evolution of Brosnan's career is also a reflection of the changing landscape of the entertainment industry. From the golden age of network television to the blockbuster era of high-budget films and the current digital revolution, he has remained a constant presence. His ability to adapt to different mediums—whether on the stage, in traditional film, or through streaming platforms—demonstrates a remarkable flexibility and forward-thinking mindset. This adaptability has allowed him to stay relevant even as the modes of storytelling have shifted dramatically over the years. For future actors and filmmakers, Brosnan's career serves as a blueprint for longevity: one must be willing to learn, to pivot, and to embrace new opportunities as they arise.

Beyond his acting achievements, Brosnan's legacy is also defined by his off-screen contributions. His commitment to environmental causes, charitable work, and humanitarian efforts have further underscored his belief in using his influence for the greater good. These endeavors reveal a man who is not only dedicated to his craft but also deeply aware of the social and environmental challenges facing the world. Brosnan's advocacy work and philanthropy have become an integral part of his public persona, illustrating that his impact extends far beyond the confines of cinema. He has shown that true success is measured not only by the accolades one receives but also by the positive changes one helps to effect in the world.

In reflecting on his storied career, many of Brosnan's peers and critics have remarked on his ability to balance the demands of fame with a grounded, sincere approach to life. His natural charm and on-screen magnetism have often been cited as key factors in his success, yet it is his humility and willingness to confront his own vulnerabilities that have truly endeared him to audiences worldwide. Whether discussing the nuances of a challenging role or the lessons learned from personal setbacks, Brosnan's insights resonate because they are born of lived experience and a deep-seated passion for storytelling.

Moreover, Brosnan's career is a testament to the power of perseverance. In an industry known for its fleeting nature, he has managed to maintain a steady presence by continuously evolving and refusing to be boxed in by a single identity. His journey is one of constant reinvention—an actor who has not only adapted to the changing tastes of audiences but has also pushed the boundaries of what is expected of a leading man. His reflections on his own work often emphasize the importance of taking risks, learning from failure, and ultimately finding joy in the process of creation.

Ultimately, the legacy of Pierce Brosnan is one of inspiration. His storied career serves as a reminder that the path to greatness is rarely linear. It is a tapestry woven from both moments of spectacular success and periods of quiet reflection and personal struggle. For future actors, his journey offers a roadmap for navigating the highs and lows of a long career in entertainment. It is a narrative defined by resilience, artistic integrity, and an unyielding commitment to evolving as a performer. In every role he has taken—from the iconic James Bond to a quirky character in an offbeat indie film—Brosnan has left an imprint on the fabric of modern cinema.

As we look back on his achievements, it is clear that his influence will continue to shape the industry for years to come. Future generations of actors and filmmakers will undoubtedly draw on the lessons of his career—embracing versatility, persevering in the face of adversity, and always striving for authenticity in their work. Pierce Brosnan's journey is not just a chronicle of his own life, but a beacon for all who dare to dream, to take risks, and to redefine what it means to be a true artist in a constantly changing world.

conclusion

Throughout his illustrious career, Pierce Brosnan has emerged not only as an iconic actor but also as a transformative force in the world of cinema and beyond. His journey—from a determined young actor in Ireland and on the London stage to a global film superstar—reflects a remarkable blend of talent, resilience, and reinvention that has captivated audiences for decades.

Brosnan's early years, steeped in the rich cultural tapestry of Ireland and later honed in the competitive environment of London's theater scene, laid a strong foundation for his future in acting. His breakthrough came with the television series Remington Steele—a role that not only showcased his innate charm and versatility but also redefined the archetype of the leading man for modern audiences. In Remington Steele, Brosnan transformed a fictional persona into a living, breathing character, displaying a rare combination of wit, vulnerability, and sophisticated magnetism that would become his signature. This role was instrumental in paving the way for his eventual casting as

James Bond—a character he reimagined for a new era with films like GoldenEye, Tomorrow Never Dies, The World Is Not Enough, and Die Another Day.

His portrayal of Bond signified more than just stepping into a legacy role; it was a reinvention of the spy genre. Brosnan's Bond was an amalgam of classic charm and modern sensibility—suave yet occasionally introspective, action-packed yet emotionally grounded. This fresh take not only reinvigorated the franchise but also influenced future interpretations of the character. The success of these films helped solidify his status as one of Hollywood's most bankable and versatile stars, enabling him to break free from typecasting and explore a wide spectrum of roles in diverse genres.

Beyond Bond, Brosnan continued to defy expectations by embracing a variety of roles that demonstrated his willingness to take risks and challenge himself artistically. In films like The Thomas Crown Affair and Dante's Peak, he moved fluidly between the worlds of high-society heists and disaster thrillers, proving that his talent extended far beyond the confines of espionage. Whether he was playing a refined art thief with a mysterious edge or a dedicated scientist confronting nature's fury, Brosnan consistently delivered performances that combined physical presence with nuanced emotion. His ability to switch seamlessly between dramatic intensity and light-hearted charm has become a benchmark for actors who seek longevity in a rapidly evolving industry.

Simultaneously, his ventures into other genres—ranging from the musical escapades in Mamma Mia! to the dark, offbeat humor of The Matador and even his foray into the superhero realm with Black Adam—attest to his relentless pursuit of creative reinvention. Each role, no matter how unconventional, has served as a building block in the multifaceted career of an actor who refuses to be defined by a single persona. This diversity has not only broadened his appeal to a wide range of audiences but has also inspired future generations of actors to embrace versatility and artistic exploration.

Off the screen, Brosnan's impact extends into his personal life and philanthropic endeavors. His family life with Keely Shaye Smith and their children has provided him with a stable, grounding influence amid the highs and lows of Hollywood's ever-changing landscape. The bonds he has nurtured with his family have served as a source of strength and inspiration, allowing him to maintain a genuine and relatable public persona despite the pressures of fame.

Perhaps most notably, Brosnan's commitment to environmental activism and philanthropy underscores a legacy that transcends cinema. Whether working to raise awareness about critical issues such as plastic pollution and marine conservation or actively participating in campaigns that support cancer research and children's health, his dedication to making the world a better place has left an indelible mark. His efforts in these areas illustrate that true influence is measured not only by box office success or critical acclaim but also by the positive change one can effect in society.

Today, Pierce Brosnan stands as a testament to the power of reinvention, resilience, and relentless creativity. His storied career has reshaped modern cinema, inspiring countless actors to challenge traditional roles and explore the full spectrum of their artistic potential. His influence is evident not only in the enduring popularity of the characters he has portrayed but also in the evolving standards of what it means to be a leading man in the 21st century.

In reflection, the life and contributions of Pierce Brosnan embody a blend of artistic excellence, personal integrity, and social responsibility. He has consistently pushed the boundaries of his craft, leaving an indelible legacy that will inspire future generations both on and off the screen. As the industry continues to change and new voices emerge, Brosnan's journey serves as a powerful reminder that true artistry is timeless—resilient in the face of adversity, ever-evolving, and always rooted in a deep, enduring commitment to both one's craft and one's community.

Ultimately, the legacy of Pierce Brosnan is not confined to any single role or achievement. It is a rich tapestry woven from decades of bold choices, transformative performances, and heartfelt contributions to society. From his breakthrough on television to his iconic portrayal of James Bond, and from his diverse film roles to his impactful advocacy work, Brosnan has proven that an actor's true influence is measured by the ability to touch lives, challenge norms, and inspire future generations. In every sense, his life and career are a celebration of artistic passion, personal courage, and a profound commitment to making a difference in the world.

Filmography

Films

- Late 1970s – Early 1980s

- Murphy's Stroke (1979) – One of Brosnan's early appearances on screen.

- The Long Good Friday (1980) – Brief role contributing to his early film work.

- The Mirror Crack'd (1980) – A supporting part in this mystery thriller.

- Mid-1980s

- The Fourth Protocol (1987) – Brosnan starred as a key operative in this Cold War thriller.

- The Deceivers (1988) – Featured in this espionage drama that further established his on-screen presence.

- Late 1980s – Early 1990s

- Noble House (1988, TV Miniseries) – Brosnan's work in a multi-episode adaptation highlighting his versatility.

- Around the World in 80 Days (1989, TV Miniseries) – Another notable early role on television adapted for the big screen format.

- Mrs. Doubtfire (1993) – Played a supporting role in this beloved family comedy.

- The Lawnmower Man (1992) – Featured in this early sci-fi film exploring virtual reality themes.

- James Bond Era

- GoldenEye (1995) – Brosnan's breakout film as James Bond, redefining the character for a new generation.

- Tomorrow Never Dies (1997) – Continued his tenure as Bond, balancing high-octane action with subtle emotional depth.

- The World Is Not Enough (1999) – Further developed the modern Bond persona with complex interpersonal nuances.

- Die Another Day (2002) – His final outing as Bond, blending traditional elements with futuristic spectacle.

- Diversifying Roles Beyond Bond

• Mars Attacks! (1996) – A foray into Tim Burton's quirky, satirical science fiction comedy.

• Dante's Peak (1997) – Portrayed a dedicated volcanologist in this disaster thriller, showcasing his ability to handle physical and emotional challenges.

• Grey Owl (1999) – Starred in the biopic of Archibald Belaney, an early conservationist known as Grey Owl.

• The Thomas Crown Affair (1999) – Played the suave, enigmatic art thief in a modern heist film that reimagined the classic tale.

• After the Sunset (2004) – Featured in this light-hearted action-comedy.

• Laws of Attraction (2004) – Took on the role of a conflicted character in this romantic comedy-drama.

• The Matador (2005) – Portrayed a disillusioned hitman in this dark comedy that received critical praise for its offbeat tone.

- Seraphim Falls (2006) – Starred in this Western epic, further demonstrating his versatility.

- Butterfly on a Wheel (2007) – Appeared in this thriller that mixed psychological tension with action.

- Mamma Mia! (2008) – Embraced a musical romantic comedy role as Sam Carmichael, displaying his lighter, playful side.

- The Ghost Writer (2010) – Delivered a nuanced performance in this political thriller directed by Roman Polanski.

- Percy Jackson & the Olympians: The Lightning Thief (2010) – Provided voice work in this adaptation of the popular fantasy series.

- The Foreigner (2017) – Took on a role in this action-thriller, contributing to his continued presence in major film projects.

- Black Adam (2022) – Entered the superhero realm by portraying Kent

Nelson/Doctor Fate, showcasing his gravitas in a high-profile franchise.

Television

- Breakthrough Role

- Remington Steele (1982–1987) – The television series that catapulted Brosnan to international fame as the titular con man turned detective.

- Other Television Work

- Nancy Astor (1982) – A miniseries that contributed to his early recognition in the United States.

- Running Wilde (1992) – A pilot for NBC in which he starred as a reporter; although the series was not picked up, it is part of his television legacy.

- Night Watch (1993) – A TV film where Brosnan explored the thriller genre outside of his work on Remington Steele.

Awards and Honors

Over a career spanning nearly five decades, Pierce Brosnan has earned widespread acclaim for his work on screen and off. His awards and honors reflect not only his contributions as an actor in both television and film but also his philanthropic efforts and commitment to environmental causes. Here is an overview of the major accolades and recognitions that have defined his career:

Industry Recognition

Brosnan's body of work has garnered several nominations and awards from some of the world's most prestigious institutions. Early in his career, his portrayal of characters in television productions such as Nancy Astor earned him critical notice and a Golden Globe nomination for Best Supporting Actor in a Miniseries or Motion Picture Made for Television. These early accolades laid the foundation for the recognition he would receive later as his career expanded.

His transformation into the iconic James Bond brought with it a wave of international attention. Brosnan's interpretation of 007 in films like GoldenEye and Tomorrow Never Dies was widely praised for its blend of classic Bond sophistication and a contemporary emotional depth. Although the Bond films are more often celebrated as box-office successes than for awards per se, his performance contributed to an enduring legacy that influenced how the character was perceived by audiences and critics alike.

Major Award Nominations and Wins

- Golden Globe Awards:

Brosnan has been nominated for several Golden Globe Awards over the years. His work in early television and his role in The Matador helped cement his reputation as an actor capable of both dramatic and comedic brilliance. While he has not always taken home the award, these nominations highlight his consistent ability to deliver engaging, memorable performances.

- Saturn Awards:

In recognition of his work in genre films, Brosnan has been honored by the Saturn Awards—instituted by the Academy of Science Fiction, Fantasy and Horror Films. For his role as Bond in Tomorrow Never Dies, he received nominations acknowledging his contributions to modern action cinema.

- Empire Awards and Blockbuster Entertainment Awards:

Brosnan's portrayal of James Bond in GoldenEye and his continued performance in subsequent films earned him accolades from critics' circles and industry awards alike. These awards celebrated his ability to bring a blend of charm, wit, and toughness to one of cinema's most enduring characters.

Honorary and Lifetime Achievement Awards

Beyond competitive awards, Brosnan's career has been celebrated through honorary recognitions that acknowledge his influence on the film industry:

- Irish Film and Television Academy (IFTA) Lifetime Achievement Award:

In recognition of his extensive contributions to Irish cinema and his influence on international film, Brosnan was honored with the IFTA Lifetime Achievement Award. This accolade underscores his role as one of Ireland's most prominent cultural ambassadors, whose work has transcended national boundaries.

- Hollywood Walk of Fame:

Brosnan's star on the Hollywood Walk of Fame stands as a testament to his enduring impact on the entertainment industry. This permanent honor celebrates not only his cinematic achievements but also his contributions as a producer and philanthropist.

- Honorary OBE (Officer of the Order of the British Empire):

In 2003, Brosnan was appointed an honorary OBE in recognition of his "outstanding contribution to the British film industry." Though he is Irish by birth and later became an American citizen, this honor underscores his significance within the broader Commonwealth cultural sphere and highlights the respect he commands in the United Kingdom.

- Honorary Degrees:

Brosnan's impact extends into academia as well. He has received honorary degrees from institutions such as the Dublin Institute of Technology and University College Cork. These academic honors acknowledge not only his artistic achievements but also his role as a public figure who has contributed to cultural and philanthropic initiatives.

Philanthropic and Advocacy-Related Honors

Brosnan's influence is not limited to the screen; his commitment to environmental activism and charitable endeavors has also earned him recognition from various organizations:

- Environmental Awards:

His long-standing work in environmental advocacy—often in partnership with his wife, Keely Shaye Smith—has been recognized by environmental groups and sustainability foundations. Awards celebrating his efforts to promote marine conservation, oppose harmful industrial practices, and support sustainable development reflect his dedication to using his celebrity for global good.

- Humanitarian and Charity Awards:

Brosnan's involvement with UNICEF and other charitable organizations has led to honors that recognize his commitment to improving children's lives and promoting health awareness. His philanthropic work, including support for cancer research and education initiatives, has resonated with fans and peers alike, highlighting a legacy that goes well beyond his film career.

Impact on Future Generations

Perhaps one of the most significant aspects of Brosnan's awards and honors is their role in inspiring future actors and filmmakers.

His career—a blend of high-profile roles, creative risk-taking, and a commitment to social causes—serves as a roadmap for emerging talent. By consistently choosing roles that challenge him and by maintaining a strong moral and ethical stance in his off-screen endeavors, Brosnan has become a role model. His accolades, whether competitive awards or honorary recognitions, are not just marks of personal achievement; they are symbols of the broader impact his work has had on the cultural landscape.

In sum, the awards and honors bestowed upon Pierce Brosnan reflect a career defined by artistic excellence, versatility, and a commitment to using his influence for positive change. From his early nominations in television to his recognition as one of the most iconic figures in modern cinema, every accolade has contributed to a rich, multifaceted legacy. These honors celebrate not only his ability to captivate audiences through memorable performances but also his broader contributions as an advocate for environmental sustainability and humanitarian causes.

As future generations of actors look to navigate the complexities of a rapidly evolving entertainment industry, they will undoubtedly find in Brosnan's achievements—and in the awards and honors that recognize them—a powerful reminder that true success is measured not only by box-office numbers or critical acclaim but also by the lasting impact one has on society. Through his work, both on and off the screen, Pierce Brosnan has set an enduring standard for excellence, creativity, and social responsibility, ensuring that his legacy will continue to inspire and guide those who follow in his footsteps.

Printed in Dunstable, United Kingdom

67044023R00087